a modicum *of* solace

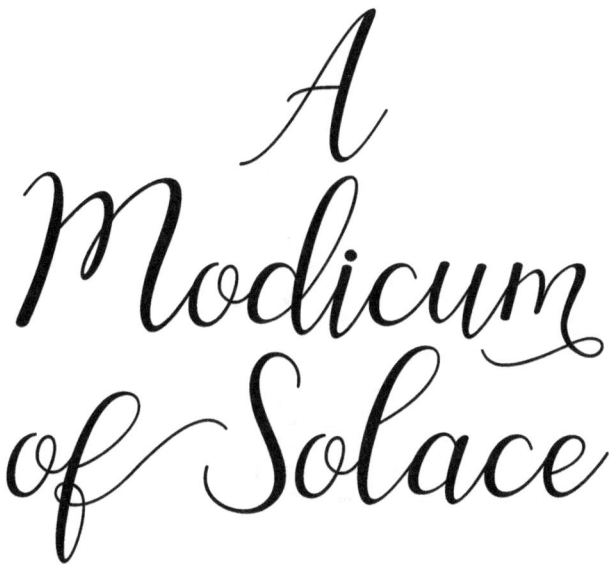

ONE WOMAN'S POLITICAL DESPAIR

SUE ROBIN, M.A.

Palmetto Publishing Group
Charleston, SC

A Modicum of Solace
Copyright © 2019 by Sue Robin
All rights reserved

No portion of this book may be reproduced, stored in a retrieval system, or transmitted in any form by any means–electronic, mechanical, photocopy, recording, or other except for brief quotations in printed reviews, without prior permission of the author.

First Edition

Printed in the United States

ISBN-13: 978-1-64111-648-0
ISBN-10: 1-64111-648-X

Dedicated to all those around the world who fight for democracy and human rights. May your dreams be realized.

Introduction

I have voted in every election since turning twenty-one. There were winners and losers in those fifty years, but until Number 45 was elected in November of 2016 I have never felt the despair and anguish for my country that washed over me. The pain roiled in my heart and then demanded to be let out. In the years since 45's election many poems have poured through my heart and out my fingers providing a modicum of solace. Mueller's appointment held me captive to hope. I waited like Godot, for an unseen man who held our country in his palm. Several men went to jail, many others were indicted. 45's people claimed victory though obstruction of justice was delineated. Now yet another incident has forced the hand of Congress to investigate a possible impeachment. I do not gloat nor take joy in this turn of events, but I know it is the ethical thing to do. Even postulating that the Senate might not impeach him, I will continue to write and to pray that good will triumph over evil.

Table of Contents

A Bit of Ugliness	1
In the Name of God and Allah	2
Left, Right and Center	3
Who Let the Dogs Out?	4
A Few Good Quotes	7
Mr. Sandman	12
It Will Take A Lifetime	13
One Can Only Hope	15
Sleep Evades Me	17
When in Rome	18
Read My Heart	20
My Entire Retirement Fund	21
The Skyline Street Walker	22
Johnny Appleseed	23
Even the Pebbles Are Crying	24
Godot	25
The Trumpettes	26
Happy Birthday to Me!	28
Ode to Seventy	31
Just Another Slice	33
Jacaranda Blue	35
America The Beautiful	36
Nowhere to Hide	37
Bellicose Banter	38

Hugh Hefner	39
The Ugly American on Steroids	40
Coping skills	42
My Heart Hurts	43
A Bad, Bad Pic	44
A Rosary of Death	45
The Muddy Water	46
A Power Grab	48
To Let Truth Win Out	49
Piles	50
Just Above My Heart	51
Will Justice Prevail	52
Acknowledgements	55

A Bit of Ugliness

To read the news on a daily basis makes us all like Sisyphus
We no sooner hear good cheer when an
onslaught of world ills assaults us
Murder, rape, drugs, wars in distant
lands and the congressional ones
Archbishops who protect pedophiles instead of children
Wonder what the world would be like if
all that was printed was good news?
Would that spawn more good news?
Gifted child sings arias at 10 years of age!
Doctor reports that Mrs. Smith is cancer free!
Neighbors join to clear trash and plant trees!
Good Samaritan rescues family from burning home!
The ultimate newspaper would contain 90% good news
A crossword puzzle, comics, and buried
deep inside a bit of ugliness
One needs the bleak to appreciate the blessings

02/08/2013

In the Name of God and Allah

We read
We watch
We feel
Each death, each lost limb
The explosions
The hate
Murders and bombs
Countries torn apart
Cities decimated
Families bereft
Little ones, aged ones
Covered in blood
All in the name of God and Allah

02/09/2013

Left, Right and Center

Left, right and center
The greatest country in the world has slipped
We are still first in something
The number of incarcerated citizens
What is wrong with this picture?
Liberals blame conservatives and
They return the favor
No longer are there conversations, or consensus
No longer is there real news for the masses
Murders and car chases, celebs and sports fill the airwaves
People watch "reality tv" rather than be real in their own lives
American movies have become remakes of remakes
Politicians look to save their jobs, not the country
And I cry

02/10/2013

Who Let the Dogs Out?

"We the people." Our Constitution starts with those words, laying forth a path to protect our rights and create a more perfect union. With Mr. Trump to guide this union we have proven to the world that we have lost our way. With each tweet I weep, and the world weeps with me.

This President fills me with dread on a daily, sometimes hourly, basis. When President Obama was elected, I felt elated because this country had elected a Black Man and, perhaps, this would be a turning point in race relations. The pendulum had swung towards inclusiveness making this world a better place.

Now Mr. Trump, with the backing of the Republican Party, has swung the pendulum back to a time of hatred. His rhetoric has emboldened the white supremacists and the Neo Nazis. They have come out of the darkness to splash swastikas on walls, send Muslim Mosques hate mail, and assault people of color, gays, Jews and immigrants. The Anti-Defamation League counted 800 antisemitic incidents in the first few months of his Presidency. The increase was frightening and ugly and has continued with his silent blessing.

In 1941 my parents found some LA neighborhoods with signs that proclaimed "NO JEWS, DOGS OR &?#$%^S". They found a place in a Jewish enclave in Boyle Heights. When I was three, they moved to the Valley. We were the only Jews on the block. Mrs. De Stefano circulated a petition to rid the street of the blight of the one

Jewish family. Fortunately, our other neighbors were good-hearted people and refused to sign.

Born in 1947 I saw many horrific newsreels of the emaciated survivors when the concentration camps were liberated, with piles of bones and clothing in the background. I would hide my eyes, but that first second was seared into my brain for eternity.

A nightmare followed me through childhood of the Nazis coming for my family. My mother would comfort me and assure me that won't happen here. She must be turning over in her grave.

My first high school crush was a boy named Mike. We had three weeks of teen age bliss until his parents found out and, through sad eyes, he told me we had to break up because I was Jewish.

My first week in college was ghastly. The young women next door followed me into the shower. Their reason: their pastor had told them that Jews had a tail and horns and they wanted to see for themselves. The next weeks weren't much better. To top off this ugly beginning to college, my dearest friend who had convinced me to attend SDS in the first place as she was excited to join the sorority her sisters had belonged to and promised she would pledge me once she was in, told me six weeks into the semester that she would not be able to invite me because I was Jewish and she rapidly disappeared from my life.

Then there was the man who thought because I went on a date with him that I would want to have sex with him. I ran out of the apartment and half- way down the driveway before he grabbed me around the neck and poured a pot of water over me. I escaped.

Now fifty years later the President is a man who has talked about grabbing women by the p@##$, makes fun of people who are different, calls women pigs and other vile things, has sent immigrants running and has taken on a cabinet that includes an avowed racist, an anti-Semite, a woman who has no knowledge of public schools with a religious agenda, a man who has a reputation for embracing conspiracy theories and another who feels left leaning Jews are no better than the Jews who aided the Nazis. I cried when I heard that.

The most consistent thing about this President is that he lies. He treats our allies with disdain and then praises Putin and Kim Jong Un. The list of sins is long, and each transgression brings a sense of bewilderment and despair. Hatred has let the dogs out, otherness has let the dogs out, and bigotry has let the dogs out. We must refuse to let hate win. Though it is incredibly hard to love the haters we cannot become what we abhor. We must protect each other. We cannot let hate win or we all lose.

February 2017

A Few Good Quotes

Just read a few quotes from FDR and wondered
aloud how my parents ever voted for him,

But that was before the internet and many things
did not come to light in the moment.

His Anti-Semitism and anti-immigrant
feelings were ugly and pervasive.

Mom and Dad did not want me to buy a
VW because of its Hitler connection.

Yet, the car they drove to California and the one they
bought for me twenty-two years later were Fords.

Henry Ford was known for being in bed with the Nazis.

Sleeping around is never a good idea.

We did not go to Knott's Berry Farm when I was
a child because the owners were John Birchers.

They were another group of Americans who thought if you
were not lily white and Christian you did not belong here.

How sad I am to see how little things
have changed since the 50s!

And still progress has been made, things are not the same.

It is a slow steady climb up a rather steep slope, with
a few steps up, and a few too many slips back.

For me the political scene today feels like
we have fallen down the mountain

We are fighting again for immigrants, for
our bodies, for the right to vote and most
importantly to see ourselves as part of the
world not the king of the world.

The ins want vouchers for our schools,
the vouchers will be minimal, the tuitions
maximal, and the children SOL.

Religion is important to them as long as it is
their religion, science not so much so.

Our beautiful land was protected from harm's way

But now those with the power have voted
for coal slag in the streams, oil pipes by the
rivers, rigs in the wilderness and the sea.

The NRA, too, has a friend in this government.

They go against common sense returning
guns to the mentally ill.

What ugliness will our society see next?

An uptick in suicides? more theatre shootings?
more school children wiped off the planet?

But then some of those in power think that
the tragedy at Sandy Hook was a hoax,
and the piles of bones from Auschwitz
were a hoax, and the American walking
on the moon, you guessed it, a hoax.

45 said repeatedly during the election that the
election was compromised. No, actually he said,
"rigged" as compromised is too big a word for him.

I believe he knew what he was talking about. He
knew about the Russians, and their involvement,
and, so yes, he was sort of speaking the truth.

But since he is a showman above all,
he uses the tricks of the trade;

Misdirection and lies.

Where will this end?

Another war? An attempt to usurp
The Constitution of the USA?

He makes enemies with ease, and,
yet, his people still love him.

Either they, too, are full of hate and fury or
perhaps they really are deplorable.

And while we may be at a nadir,

The Muslim Ban protests have let the Arab world
know how much most Americans care.

The assault on our environment has brought scientists
out of their labs into the streets in protest. Women
have put on their pussy hats and joined hands to
celebrate, and support one another, demand equal
pay, and assert control over our own bodies.

Our men have joined in, hats and all.

Whole cities have declared themselves a sanctuary zone.

Subway riders together washed away the hateful words
some Anti-Semite smeared across the windows.

Muslims raised money for the desecrated Jewish Cemetery

And Jews gave Muslims the key to their
Temple when their Mosque was burned.

All across this vast and beautiful county good deeds abound.

Humor has twittered across the internet
playfully taking down the ugliness.

Political engagement is strong and brings
hope that we can survive the utter chaos.

To begin again marching back up the mountain
toward civility, healing and progress.

Mr. Sandman

Night after night I lie awake waiting
for Mr. Sandman to arrive.
He is missing in action.
The only one who raps on the door is the orange man who
sneers and throws temper tantrums far better than a child.
Either he lies in wait while I brush, floss, take my
meds and do my "sleep well" Gi gong or he finds
me at 3 am with my heart broken and my head
swimming in the pain of his latest appointment.
Even an Ativan can't make him leave.
Like a lover who has betrayed me I want him out
of my bedroom, out of my life, but he is neither a
former lover nor, has he in truth, betrayed me.
He has done exactly what he said he would. He
drained the swamp, only to put them in his cabinet.
I beg for sleep and sweet dreams of a better time.
But his insinuation into my brain wreaks its own havoc

January 2017

It Will Take A Lifetime

Years of draught and now four inches
of rain in a day and a half
On a street nearby a sinkhole ate two cars
Rivers replaced roads
Freeways shut down
The wind then joined hands with the rain
Pulled trees up by their roots
Hurled them at an apartment building
at one end of the city and
Took out six cars in one fell swoop in another
At least one person was washed away and
another, a child, crushed beneath a tree
Here atop our mountain, no worry of a flood
The electricity flickered on and off more than
once, but decided to keep us company
The storm has moved on
There is in its wake, however, no cable
No internet, no "Words with Friends"
A blessing and a curse
The newspaper arrived in the morning we drank
our tea, did the crossword and Sudoku
Read the horrors of the day, but
Since that time the world may have ended for all we know
The first night Andres Bocelli sang us to sleep

The next we listened to the UCLA/SC game on the radio!
In the evening Itzaak Perlman fiddled for us
We have endured no Trump tantrums
(though I am sure they happened)
It was peaceful without his nightly assault
on our first amendment rights
Alas, his image is seared into my brain and breaks my heart
Two days without him was lovely, but
the fear has not dissipated
It will take a lifetime for that

02/19/2017

One Can Only Hope

The rains have come at last, and like all things it
has brought mother nature's bounty and wrath

The grass is a delicate green that one sees
after the earth has been nourished,

But in the verdant glow a tree or two has
fallen, wires are down, mud slides undermine
the hills, and someone has lost their home,
and another has been swept away

The pendulum swings, but at a cost

Uncle Sam is just as fickle and unpredictable

For eight years we, here in America,
dined on grace and diplomacy

A slow, steady fatherly hand brought
us back from the brink

But those who hid their ugly stripes
are now in the cat bird seat

The daily fair is lies, hatred and
misdirection under a cloud of fear

One can only hope the arc of life will
once again find its center

02/21/2017

Sleep Evades Me

They come in the middle of the night
Terror washes through my heart and sleep evades me
They have taken over the White House and my bedroom
Edicts filled with hate and stupidity
Guns for the mentally ill, coal slag in the waters,
Immigrants, the life blood of our nation, banned
Gynecologists' orders replaced by politicians' laws
The wolves are in charge of the hens
They have eaten away at my peace
Tears flow, anger boils and I wait in my pink pussy hat
And wonder if justice will triumph

02/2017

When in Rome

Madame Le Pen goes to Lebanon to broaden her
foreign policy experience, but refuses to wear a
head scarf, and is not admitted to the meeting.

Her choice, and the consequences will
be hers to endure as well.

She must not have learned, "When in
Rome do as the Romans do".

At twenty-one I traipsed across Europe
on a Eurail-Pass for three months.

Able at long last to see the sculptures that had been
flashed slide by slide before my eyes in Art History.

The art works were strewn across the continent in
museums, in the public squares and in the churches.

I was forewarned that to enter the magnificent
Cathedrals I must cover my head and arms
and pants were verboten for women.

I did not hesitate. I knew covering my
body was an act of respect.

It would not convert me. I am a Jew, but I
am a Jew who honors all religions as I am
sure Jesus did, for he, too, was a Jew.

My sweetheart is a Catholic and he has been to Bar
Mitzvahs, weddings and funerals with my family and
gently places the kipah on his head out of respect.

Some temples require the removal of one's shoes.
Others the men cover their heads. Jews wear tallit and
tzitzits. Muslims have their prayer rug and hijab.

When I am in Rome, I eat the foods of the country,
read about their culture, religions and art and, most
importantly, bring my heart to meet theirs

I am afraid that Le Pen must have left hers at home.

2/23/2017

Read My Heart

Read my heart
It is out for all to see
Right there on my sleeve
Injustice makes my nose flair
Defaced gravestones have me in tears
A man killed because of his birthplace
Brings me to my knees
A slogan that is beyond ugly
leaves me speechless
The irony is not lost
Wearing a sweatshirt that calls for lynching a journalist
Is covered under the first amendment
Yet the wearer wants to eviscerate the freedom of the press.
My heart is pricked daily with pain
My head cannot comprehend such hatred
But then a smile of a total stranger
A friend's hug
A glimpse of my grandchildren at play
My son's voice on the phone
My sweetheart's tenderness
Bring me to the center
I breathe and remember what truly matters

02/27/17

My Entire Retirement Fund

The stock market is up
All those with money are ecstatic
Less regulations, less taxes
More money
Even my retirement fund is higher
But at what price?
People will be without care
The environment will suffer
Worldwide friendships will falter
All to make the rich-richer
I would give all my gains
Hell, I would give my entire retirement fund
To have clean water, air to fill my lungs,
Doctors to heal the sick and
Welcome mats instead of walls.

02/28/2017

The Skyline Street Walker

We live at the top of a hill
A third of a mile flat patch lies out front
I traipse from here to there and back again 15 times
My honey affectionately calls me the Skyline Street Walker
One neighbor inquired "don't you get bored?"
But there is a view of downtown and the lush canyon
The hawks soar and dance above me
A conversation with a neighbor opens my heart
The UPS guy stops to chat, Fed-ex, too
I know all the work crew at the remodel up the street
The realtors selling Katy's house know me by name
A constant stream of my favorite music from
Segovia to Paul Simon urge me on
And the neighborhood four legged creatures
Give me my doggie fix along the way
Tails wag, and love is freely shared
Anxiety is down, blood pressure is perfect and
Best of all, on my walk, number 45 does not exist

02/28/17

Johnny Appleseed

Johnny Appleseed brought sweet
fruit across the country, but
For the last year the orange man has
sowed instead the seeds of hate
He taunted a reporter with a medical condition
Called women pigs, the press liars,
Diminished the intelligence service
Demeaned heroes
And now those seeds have taken root
The haters who laid dormant have now sprouted
Over 100 bomb threats to Temples,
A Mosque burned to the ground
A man murdered because of his birthplace
Graves desecrated
Vile adjectives tossed at women, immigrants
and anyone not lily white
Then he reads one speech from a teleprompter.
Undoubtedly, one written by someone else
Manages not to tweet for 24 hours
And everyone says, "Look! He is Presidential!"
But I want to remind the world that
One cannot change the tiger's stripes
Nor the bull's shit

March 2, 2017

Even the Pebbles Are Crying

Little children maimed and murdered in their beds,
Mothers and fathers gone
Sister and brothers, too
People wander in a haze of fear
War has taken over an entire country
Bombs and gas fill the sky
Homes and hospitals lie in rubble
The screams of a nation are heard around the world
Their tears flood the streets and even the pebbles are crying

04/26/17

Godot

The coyotes yipped and yowled just as
I crawled under the covers.
I do not feel threatened by the noise.
It blends well with my honey's snores.
Even without the din, sleep is not easy to come by these days.
The nightmare in the White House would rather build
the egos of Nazis than save the lives of Dreamers.
He pardons an outright racist, not to
mention putting some in his cabinet.
Anything that Obama touched is to be wiped away as if
that will make O's legacy disappear or his own shine.
He toys with war with a maniac,
Tearing the peaceful fabric of our world to shreds.
This is what gnaws at me day and night.
I am reminded of one scene in Beckett's
play "Waiting for Godot"
One man contemplates suicide and other absurdities
The actors talk and wait and wait for an unseen person
While in our world an outrageous man
pretends to lead the country
And Like those characters I wait and wait
not for Godot, but for Mr. Mueller.

05/2017

The Trumpettes

He is gone for a few days.
I, alone in the house.
All is serene.
No tv with its constant drone.
I am doing all the same things we do together.
Breakfast at Joan's,
The wait staff a bit friendlier then when we are two.
Trader Joe's for milk, lettuce and five other
things that jumped into the cart.
A five mile walk out front.
Chats with the neighbors.
Laundry and dishes.
I iron and cut out a pattern.
There is an emptiness though.
I imagine this is what it might be like
If he were to die.
He is often downstairs and I up,
But now he is nowhere to be found.
Two days business in Tulsa,
Five days with his brother and family in Denver.
I would not go this time, declined the invite.
Twenty family members who thought
Trump was a good idea.
Broke my heart and the choice, though painful, was easy.

Peace and quiet here or the slurs and arrows of Trumpettes.
Or worse still my own anger and
resentment spilling into the ethers.
No need to melt the snowflake with heated
arguments that would only lead to despair.
I am content being one of the many delicate snowflakes,
unique and, yet, alike, truly quite beautiful.
We are known for standing up for the downtrodden.
Which in the end is quite preferred to kicking the stool
out from under or watching 45 shove a world leader,
And congratulate a despot on the great job he has done.
Or Mrs. 45 slap at his hand,
Or see The Pope frown
Or a politician assault a reporter,
Or yet another Russian connection.

05/27/17

Happy Birthday to Me!

On this, my natal anniversary, I muse about what
it means to be on this blue dot for 70 years.

This orb with all manner of life continues
to stun me with its magnificence.

The play of light and shadow on the
hillsides, the dew on the flora.

The hawks that soar and squawk at the
crack of dawn as I sip my tea.

Perhaps I will birth a poem later,
imagine fertility at this ripe age!

I began celebrating this auspicious occasion last weekend.

Meals and movies with the ones that
write joy all over my heart.

The movies all suited to the under nine crowd, and a lovely
food fest: Pad Thai, sushi, congee and a little lox and bagels
to remind me of my roots. Not all at once, mind you!

Walked twenty miles over several days, played a bit of
catch and helped the dolly's change their clothes.

Seventy years seems old to me, though I do not feel old.

At twenty-one I traveled through Europe while
my father turned sixty, I wept thinking he
might not be alive when I returned home!

I am brutally aware that we humans do not come
with an expiration date printed on our bottoms, my
brother having taken leave of us all too soon.

If the stars align just right, perhaps, I will
share the glory of the grandkids' college
graduations or a wedding or two.

But one never knows, tomorrow or next
week or next year I might drop dead.

Some unknown illness, a random shooting or just
one too many political fiascos might take me out.

The takeaway from life here on earth is that we must
perform mitzvot, which is not simply a good deed,
but a way to connect to the place of inner peace. The
kindness of humanity is all around us though we are
challenged to remember it in the depths of despair.

While we are able, we are obligated to tend to our bodies, nurture mother earth, honor life in all its forms, and remember always, that love matters.

It truly does make the world go around and, more importantly, it makes it well worth living.

Happy Birthday to me.

June 16, 2017

Ode to Seventy

At seventy I swim in the vagaries of old age.
I chase stray eyebrow hairs weekly
in the fifteen times mirror,
It was a gift from my mother when I turned fifty.
That same mirror, a bit of an insult
then, and, now, a godsend.
Much more salt than pepper frames my face.
My bones creak and ache until they wiggle free of sleep.
The perky nipples are a bit further from their crest.
Eyelids and other parts as well.
Never fond of bats with their pointy
teeth and insidious ways,
But somehow their wings have taken
up residence in my arms.
The scar on my left cheek where the doc removed a mole
in my twelfth year has been joined by the ones the crow
left after he gingerly stepped on the corners of my eyes.
There are other lines, too, the ones etched
by the losses along the way.
There have been days that have crushed my heart, I
thought I would not be able to close the door on anguish.
Somehow, slowly, it has been shut, and I rise
to wonder what is behind door #2.
There are perks to this milestone,

Blessed with two grandchildren who shine a light on life,
A quiet morning interrupted only by the birdsong,
Or a sunset over the ocean,
The time to read all day if I please,
To eat breakfast at 11 or dinner at 5.
Amidst this glory, worries persist.
The mass found two years ago is gone.
Though every new pain begs me to ask, "Is it back?"
Will this life end in a flourish or a
long, drawn out pity party?
My name has not been in lights nor do I
have a book on the best seller list.
However, there is something far superior to all
of the glitz and kudos out in the world.
My son has gleaned the best from his father and me.
He moves in the world with integrity and wisdom.
True to himself, kind to the world and
deeply committed to his family.
No greater legacy exists.

06/16/2017

Just Another Slice

Driving through Phillipsburg, Montana
I pass two churches, same God
One right next door to the other
Down the street there are dueling flags, one
quite large and the other larger still
On the back of a pick-up's rear window the
entire pledge of allegiance is inscribed
This is Big Sky Country, puffy clouds fill
every corner, and lots of open spaces
Though the minds here I am not so sure
This is Trump country
The people are friendly and pleasant, but they
do not know my politics nor religion
Nor I theirs
I have been here three days and have seen only one
Black Man in a sea of rural white America
I imagine him to be as lonely as I feel
One would be hard pressed to find a
bagel with lox in this town
"Lose your way? Find Jesus" signs flit by interrupted
only by bill- boards, which proclaim with equal
fervor "Over 50? Get a colorectal exam!"
Save your soul complimented by save your ass
A doe got up close and personal with the brand- new rental car

Brakes and reflexes worked in perfect harmony
Five miles down the road our hearts have almost stopped
beating at the speed of a hummingbird's wings
Just another slice of the good old US of A

6/20/17

Jacaranda Blue

I remember at twenty-three years of age standing on a
flight of stairs at Grossinger's in the Catskill Mountains
The cacophony of Yiddish interspersed with
heavily accented English (An exact replica of
my grandmother's voice!) filled the air
An epiphany washed over me that though,
God willing, I would someday be an old Jewish
woman, I would never sound like them
Today sitting in a Missoula coffee shop
filled to the brim with elders and
Having just stared down seventy and survived
I know I will never be a dowdy old woman
with blue hair and couture by Sears
If my hair is ever dyed blue, it will be
jacaranda blue with purple streaks
And likewise, if Sears is my clothier, I will be
like the fairy God Mother in Cinderella
"Bibbity, bobbity, boo", nip and tuck and bedazzle that
gawd awful ordinary into a bit of haute couture.

6/21/2017

America The Beautiful

No easy fix
Not for the economy nor the acrimony
The politicians what to keep their jobs
Some pander to the left and others to the right
All of them do nothing well
America the beautiful is struggling
Not America the Tea Party nor America the Unions
The left hand needs to talk to the right
Come together now from sea to shining sea

07/18/2017

Nowhere to Hide

Neo Nazis: does that mean new Nazis?
What is new about the same old hate?
The fears of my youth weigh heavily upon me
A repetitive nightmare haunted my childhood
The Nazis would march down Costello Avenue
I would run to my parent's bed and crawl under the covers
Now the hate mongers are marching for real
In Charlottesville, Berkley and Phoenix
Mom and Dad are long gone
And I have nowhere to hide.

08/14/2017

Bellicose Banter

In the hall dedicated to peace,
He proffers bellicose banter.
Like an ill taught child, he taunts a mad man.
They are two peas in a pod;
Each threatening bombs and genocide.
Neither willing to talk, both posturing.
Boastful tit for tat.
The old male version of mine is bigger than yours:
Fish, hands or other body parts,
Though brains are definitely left out of this equation.
Shall we build bomb shelters again? Hide under desks?
Or pray that there is a direct hit, and we die quickly
Before the fallout oozes across the country?

09/20/2017

Hugh Hefner

Hugh Hefner died
My first instinct was good riddance
He has done more to objectify women
than any other living being
I was reminded though of his cutting-edge
efforts to publish Black authors and
His insistence that his clubs be integrated
at a time when that was still a dream
The reality is like the rest of humanity
A few rays of sunshine amidst a dreadful storm

9/28/2017

The Ugly American on Steroids

Bomb threats at temples
Mosques burned and defiled
Number 45 remains inarticulate
His strings being pulled by a man who wants
the country as we know it to end
I am flooded, frazzled and in disbelief
Almost two years since 45 was elected
It seems like an eternity
I remain filled with despair, anguish and now disgust
Our country's values highjacked by an idiot
He lambasts the immigrants while standing
next to his immigrant wife,
While at Mar a Largo they look for visas for workers.
He plays to the lowest common
denominator: the hatred of the 'other'
#45 has just returned from a European trip
He managed to berate Chancellor Merkel
for making a deal with Russia
Then insulted PM May and indicated that
Boris would make a real good PM
Our allies in NATO were not spared his abuse
The idea of diplomacy hidden under a rock
He denigrates our national security team,
our senators and our country

Russia's meddling has been known about since 2016
He does not believe it
Then this narcissistic Cheeto has the
chutzpah to cozy up to Putin
The public speculates Russia must have something on him
Whores and golden showers, porn
stars and playboy models?
But money, laundered or otherwise, seems a bit more likely
He continues to claim no collusion, he won the
election hugely, though many indictments, several
guilty pleas and more trials to come beg to differ.
And still he does not believe it
But to misquote Shakespeare "The bad guy
dost protest too much, me thinks."

October 2017

Coping skills

Amidst the fear and panic of life,
We humans find ways to muddle through.
The PhDs call them coping skills.
We all have them.
Some considered healthy, others not so much.
There are those who stuff their bellies
and then their feelings,
Others hide behind the booze or Maryjane.
I find a bit of silliness lightens my load.
Love does wonders to heal the soul,
Music and poetry, too.
Patience helps us to endure the painful.
And sometimes an indictment comes
along at just the right moment.

10/30/2017

My Heart Hurts

My heart hurts.
Two little girls are dead.
One 14, the age Moore's accuser was when he raped her.
The other 10, the age of my awesome grandson.
These sweet innocents were taunted into despair;
both children driven to suicide by bullies.
One teased for being tall, another for being black.
The President of the USA set the table for these horrors.
He cannot open his mouth without humiliating someone.
He demeans the North Korean dictator,
Berates the Prime Minister of Britain,
Insults the Democratic leaders,
Debases his own party,
Receives thanks for all of this from
the fascist and the Nazis,
All while our children are being buried.

12/06/2017

A Bad, Bad Pic

The man who calls himself President,
Tweets that a photo of Franken is a bad, bad pic.
When asked about his own accusers and Moore's,
He says unequivocally that since they did
not admit guilt they must not be.
He forgets that he was caught on tape
proclaiming his ability to grab women at his
pleasure because he is a really big star.
Poor Mr. Franken had to settle for pretending
to grab tits since he wasn't a really big star.
Mr. Moore wants to be elected a senator he
also states that the last time America was
great was during the time of slavery.
A Republican woman states she has to decide between
a person who approves of abortions and a pedophile.
Perhaps if she reframed the statement the choice is either
a man who acknowledges a woman's right to seek the
medical care she needs or one who thinks it appropriate
to defile children, her choice might be simpler.

01/20/2018

A Rosary of Death

They hang around my neck like beads,
Mother, brothers, friends now gone.
Each remembrance a meditation,
A rosary of death.
There is a hunger in missing someone
I want to hear my mother's laughter
And my brother's kindness,
But the news sends the beads flying,
Leaving in its place a yoke of disgust, threats
of a nuclear holocaust followed by another school shooting.
I thought by the time I reached seventy the world would find
a path to peace,
Instead hatred has been amplified.

02/18/2018

The Muddy Water

Dreamed last night that the muddy water is rising
I am desperately trying to save the children
Standing precariously on a ledge grabbing at two children
Holding their heads above water
Screaming for someone, anyone, to help save the children
All this in the wake of another school shooting
Now awake I watch the teens desperately
try to make a difference
Calling for gun reform and still the NRA rants on
More guns, guns in the hands of
teachers, all around the schools
Yes, that will do it they cry more guns
Do they own stock in the gun companies?
Is Russian imbuing them with funds?
Probably an affirmative to both
The 45th President whose bone spurs helped
him avoid the draft five times
(Though more likely his father's connections
kept him from harm's way)
Now claims he would have run into the school armed or not
The armed secret service surrounding Reagan,
and Kennedy were not able to protect them
Define militia please? a small army
Our forefathers wanted to create an army some say

it was to protect us as we fought for freedom from
England, some say to protect us from any slave uprising
Both probably a bit of truth.
There are numerous militias now: Army,
Navy, Air Force, Coast Guard, Reserves
How have we as a country morphed into a gun for
every man, woman and child and then some?
Truly if someone hunts to put food on
the table, I have no quarrels
Someone wants to do target practice okay
But an AK47? Multiple handguns, rifles and bullets
enough to kill a classroom or concert goers?
I do not understand that mentality any more
than I understand that of the killer.

March 2, 2018

A Power Grab

The head of state in China now has his job for eternity
Guess what? Number 45 wants that, too
Power grab from a man who thrives on chaos
He likes the sound of President for life
Sessions will not do everything his boss says
Only those things that jive with his own racist agenda
AG and I disagree about everything he is doing save one
He speaks truth to power and tells his Donny
I will continue to do my job with dignity
Each tweet makes me cringe and each
executive order brings a flood of tears
Now it is okay for some people to
bring elephant trophies home
Donald Jr. Perhaps?
I cannot see Mr. Mueller at work.
He works in stealth mode.
I have him encircled in light and in my prayers.
He holds the thin thread of sanity for me
Please get your man and all the little
thieves beholden to him

3/4/18

To Let Truth Win Out

I had put such hope in the Mueller Repot
Though many were sent to jail and
Obstruction of Justice was evident
The Orange Monster remains in office
Seemingly untarnished by all that transpired
Many members of his staff are doing time
Lots of indictments issued
But he still called it a witch hunt
Now impeachment is on the horizon
His spin doctors and fixers all call it overreach
He is stuck on witch hunt
I am neither gloating nor even happy at this turn
It is the ethical thing to do
I pray his Teflon coating is sufficiently scratched
To let truth win out

September 28, 2019

Piles

Walked into the bank yesterday and noted that someone's pooch
Had left a deposit
The bank greeter had been informed and had gathered
paper towels and carefully covered the mess
Cleaning it up was not part of her job description
Unlike the USAG who redacts here,
forbids interviews there,
Writes his own version of the truth
Works hard to clean up the piles his Owner has left

09/26/2019

Just Above My Heart

The bedroom is rather crowded these past few nights
My sweetheart right next to me
Laura Lee hovers just above my heart
Frank, easily seventy pounds lighter, but
still smiling, is there across the room
Both old friends placed on hospice this week
And as if that is not enough, in the
corner lurks the orange viper
Spewing venom with each tweet
I, too, flooded with memories do not sleep
And fear that the orange monster might win again

7/20/2019

Will Justice Prevail

In bed at 10, sleep mask, ear plugs, "Breathe Right" all in place
Curled up on my right side and waited for Hypnos to arrive
And watched as my mind went from
what to wear tomorrow
To the impeachment
What to pack for a trip four months from now?
To the impeachment
Maybe I should get up early and prepare meatloaf?
To the impeachment
Is a poem brewing?
To the impeachment
At eleven I take two Tylenol and a CBD pill
I slip between the covers once again
Left side, right side, on my back
I make a shopping list for dinner on Sunday
And still I lie awake
I do four calming breaths, meditate for a few moments,
Only a few because these racing thoughts keep coming
Gently hold the relaxation points for acupressure
Snippets of the impeachment hearing echo in my head

Finally, sometime a bit after one AM
I drop off to dreamland
Awake by seven AM and the damned
litany is right there waiting for me.
Will justice prevail? Will I ever sleep through the night?

11/21/2019

Acknowledgements

I am enormously grateful to Laura Lee Larsen for the friendship, love and editing skills she generously shared with me over the last thirty-eight years. She is gone now, but she will remain safe in my heart and the hearts of her many friends and dear family. I would like to offer my love and gratitude to Russ for his encouragement, and to my son and his family for their loving support. I want to thank, too, the Sherman Oaks Senior Center writing group who gave me a little push to move towards publishing my work.

www.ingramcontent.com/pod-product-compliance
Lightning Source LLC
LaVergne TN
LVHW011858060526
838200LV00054B/4407